Firewalking

Rob Waring, *Series Editor*

Australia • Brazil • Japan • Korea • Mexico • Singapore • Spain • United Kingdom • United States

T0052356

Words to Know

This story is set in northern Greece and takes place in a village called Agia Eleni [αγια ελενι].

 Firewalking. Read the paragraph. Then match each word with the correct definition.

The Anastenaria [αnαstεnαriα] is a traditional firewalking ritual annually performed in certain northern Greek villages. In each village, special shrines contain holy icons that are used in the ceremonies. On the day before a festival honoring Saint Constantine [kαnstəntin], a huge fire is lit and people gather to dance. As they move to the music of the lyre, participants enter a powerful spiritual state. Firewalkers then dance through hot coals believing that the saints will give them blessings for doing so.

1. ritual _____	**a.** a religious place that honors a holy person or object
2. shrine _____	**b.** in some religions, a religious painting of a holy person
3. icon _____	**c.** a person chosen by God in some religions
4. saint _____	**d.** a ceremony done to mark a sacred event or day
5. lyre _____	**e.** the burning or red-hot matter remaining after a fire
6. coals _____	**f.** a special type of Greek musical instrument

coals

B Christian or Pagan?

Read the paragraph. Then write the correct underlined word or phrase next to each definition.

The firewalking ritual is not fully accepted by all people, including the <u>Greek Orthodox</u> Church. Though the church does <u>worship</u> Saint Constantine, it feels that the ceremonies of the Anastenarians—or firewalkers—are more <u>pagan</u> than truly <u>Christian</u>. Church <u>priests</u> do not promote firewalking and often consider it to be <u>sacrilegious</u>.

1. show great respect for a god or gods: _____

2. showing disregard for something holy; against religious rules: _____

3. the name of the established church in Greece: _____

4. of or related to Jesus Christ and his religious teachings: _____

5. people who perform religious duties and ceremonies: _____

6. from a time before the main religions when people believed in several gods: _____

icon

modern Greek lyre

A firewalker carries the icon of a saint across the hot coals.

It is nighttime in the northern Greek village of Agia Eleni, and an annual spring festival is in progress. Greek Orthodox priests are leading a church service to worship Saint Constantine, the man responsible for bringing the Christian religion to the Roman Empire. Saint Constantine is particularly worshiped in the village of Agia Eleni, and religious icons of him are carried through the streets by the faithful during the time of the festival. Moving to the sound of a uniformed band playing music, the religious **procession**[1] snakes through the town as worshipers walk to the beat of the music.

The procession eventually ends at a local church. The Saint's icons are then returned to the religious center during a special ceremony in which priests deliver a series of religious recitations. Once the icons are safely placed within the confines of the church, worshipers line up for a chance to kiss the icons and ask for the blessing of the saint. Once they are finished, the believers **cross themselves**[2] and hurry away into the night. But when the formality of the Greek Orthodox ceremony ends, another ritual commences. This ritual is one that the church calls 'pagan' and 'sacrilegious.' It is a thousand-year-old ceremony in which practitioners test their faith with another kind of walk—a walk through fire.

---

[1] **procession:** a group of people, vehicles, etc. walking or traveling in the same manner, especially in a formal situation
[2] **cross (oneself):** make a hand movement down and across oneself as a religious act

 CD 2, Track 05

A Painting of Saint Constantine and Saint Elena in a Greek Church

For much of the year, the village of Agia Eleni is a **quaint**[3] little town with a population of just 700 people. Many of its residents, like 54-year-old **Kyriakos Patsos**,[4] feel extremely lucky to be able to live in such a beautiful rural village. Most of the time, Kyriakos lives peacefully in his house, tends his garden, rides his motorbike, and generally enjoys his life in the countryside. At festival times, though, Kyriakos changes his role, and his responsibilities lean towards something that many may consider rather unusual. He becomes the chief icon bearer for the duration of a firewalking festival called the 'Anastenaria.'

[3]**quaint:** old-fashioned and attractive
[4]**Kyriakos Patsos:** [kiriɑkɔs pætsɔs]

The Anastenaria ritual centers on a set of ancient icons that worshipers believe have special powers to heal and protect. Stories about the icons have been passed on from generation to generation. One story claims that 1,000 years ago, worshipers rescued the icons of Saint Constantine from a burning church. According to the story, the rescuers escaped from the dangerous burning flames **miraculously**[5] unharmed.

Ever since that time, the **descendants**[6] of those worshipers have carried the icons into the coals of the fire during the Anastenaria ritual to prove their faith—and to seek blessings from Saint Constantine. The festival involves believers walking over the hot ashes of burnt wood with bare feet—a practice sometimes known as 'firewalking.' Before the actual firewalking begins, however, the participants spend hours dancing to traditional music, carrying the icons in circles as they move, and practicing while they wait for their chance to walk on fire.

---

[5]**miraculously:** in a way that cannot be explained by the laws of nature

[6]**descendant:** people born from a particular family line

Identify Cause and Effect

Circle the cause and underline the effect in each of the sentences.

1. The icons were rescued from the church because the building was on fire.

2. The rescuers were unharmed by the fire, which led them to believe that the saints were protecting them.

3. Believers these days think that by carrying the icons they can prove their faith.

While its practitioners believe the Anastenaria ritual to be sacred and holy, other people, including the Greek Orthodox Church, view the ritual as sacrilege, a pagan custom that has survived from days long ago. Both the firewalking itself and risking the holy icons are thought to show disrespect. Kyriakos explains why some people are against the ceremony. "People who oppose the tradition dislike the fact that we take the icons along in the fire," he says. "That's why they claim the tradition is pagan."

Kyriakos has firewalked most of his life and he is a strong believer in the power and significance of the ritual. For others, faith came later in life—in a time of extreme need. **Sotiris Panagiotou**[7] is one of those who turned to firewalking after suffering a crisis in his life. Before his life-changing event, Sotiris explains that he had long admired the firewalkers, but never expected to do it himself—until the day that he almost lost his life.

Sotiris Panagiotou: [sɔtiris panayɔtu]

Sotiris is a car mechanic and owns his own garage. Several years of working on cars in the closed environment of his garage exposed him to dangerous **fumes**[8] that ultimately damaged his heart. Then one day at work, he suffered a heart attack and was rushed to the hospital.

Sotiris underwent emergency heart surgery in an attempt to repair the serious condition; it was an operation that is usually performed on much older patients. Sotiris was only 41 at the time. During her time of worry, Sotiris's wife lit candles in church and asked Saint Constantine to spare her husband's life. Luckily, Sortiris survived.

During the recovery period following the surgery, Sotiris attended the Anastenaria ritual. It was then that he felt a calling to walk across the hot coals. He explains what the experience was like. "I went there and I lit a candle," he says, "and while the firewalking was happening, I felt the power to take my shoes off and I joined the rest." Sotiris was unharmed by the hot coals, and since that day he has been a firewalker.

---

[8]**fume:** the gas, smoke, or odor given off by something, usually by a chemical

Not everyone feels the power of faith as strongly as Sotiris, however. At this year's festival, 72-year-old **Iro Handjantonieu**[9] wants to walk through the fire to test her faith, but does not know if she has the strength or the power of mind to do it. Iro, who lives in Athens, has attended the Anastenaria every year since 1968, but tonight will be a particularly challenging test of her faith.

As sunset approaches, worshipers build a huge fire and, with much excitement and high expectations, the ceremony begins. As always, it starts with ancient folk songs played on traditional lyres. It's powerful music that **touches the believers' hearts**[10] and moves their feelings and senses. For many of those attending the ritual, dancing is a form of **confession**.[11] As the evening progresses, guilt and other emotions can become too much for some and they begin to cry as they dance and watch. It creates a powerful spiritual atmosphere, one that affects Iro as well. She weeps as she moves through the crowd, moved to tears by the weight of her **sins**.[12]

The dancers continue their preparation for the firewalking ceremony by dancing around a small room near the festival. As they do so, Kyriakos picks up the sacred icon of Saint Constantine and moves through the group, his eyes closed in concentration as he prepares himself for his first steps across the burning coals. The saint—and the believers' faith in him—are the only protection the Anastenarians will take into the fire.

---

[9]**Iro Handjantonieu:** (irou hɑdzɑntɔniu)
[10]**touch (one's) heart:** affect one's emotions
[11]**confession:** an admission of having done something wrong, a practice that is common in Christian religions
[12]**sin:** an act against religious beliefs; something wrong or bad

Outside, the preparation for the big event continues. The fire has grown to huge proportions and has finally collapsed, forming the bed of burning coals across which the believers will walk. Back inside, the Anastenarians are now ready, and prepare by crossing themselves one last time as they pray and slowly remove their shoes and socks. While the Orthodox Church might not approve of what they're about to do, Anastenarians see firewalking as a way to receive blessings from Saint Constantine. For some, the ceremony removes them from the hierarchical structure of the church and offers an opportunity for direct communication with higher beings.

The time has come for the ancient ritual to begin. A light wind has blown across the glowing coals, making them bright and extremely hot as they are spread into a glowing circle on the earth. The firewalkers form a small procession as they leave the building near the fire, with Kyriakos at the lead. When the small group reaches the edge of the burning coals, Kyriakos pauses for a moment. He then crosses himself, kisses the icon, and looks down at the circle of fire before him. Finally, he slowly begins his dance, gracefully moving his feet first left, then right in a backwards and forwards motion. As the dance continues, Kyriakos moves closer and closer to the coals until finally he's on them. He crosses the coals quickly, keeping in motion with the music. His first pass through the fire is from the direction of north to south. He then performs a second pass, moving from east to west, his steps intended to form a symbol of a holy cross. All the while he dances, Kyriakos holds the icon of the saint closely and shows no indication of pain.

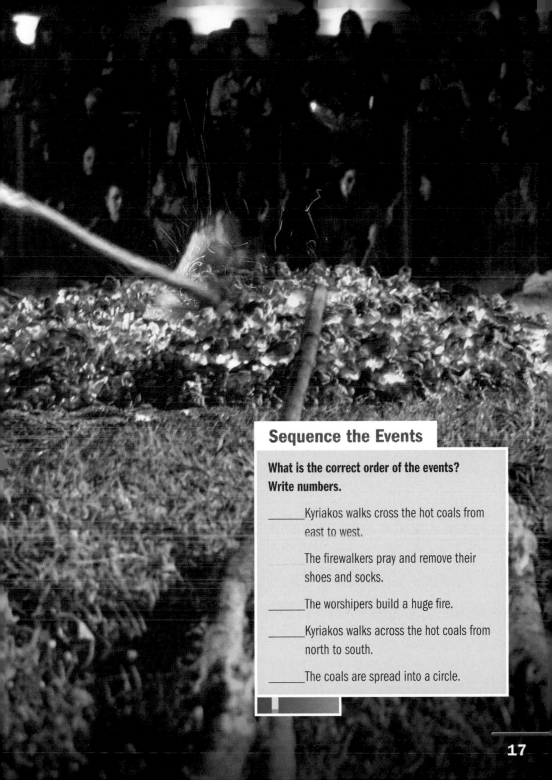

Sequence the Events

What is the correct order of the events?
Write numbers.

_____Kyriakos walks cross the hot coals from east to west.

_____The firewalkers pray and remove their shoes and socks.

_____The worshipers build a huge fire.

_____Kyriakos walks across the hot coals from north to south.

_____The coals are spread into a circle.

The spiritual act of firewalking is surrounded in mystery and analyzed by **skeptics**.[13] It is believed by most that individuals are only able to firewalk without burning themselves under certain conditions. One expert reports that there have been several cases of people trying to walk across hot coals without ceremony or ritual that have resulted in severe burns on the feet of the individuals. However, when participating in a ritual with others, a certain energy in the group is created that often elevates the spirit. This strong belief and group dynamic often result in people being able to walk across burning-hot coals without feeling pain. While little empirical data regarding the issue exists, there may be something about this group energy that prevents firewalkers from getting burned.

Back in Agia Eleni, the followers of Saint Constantine continue their ritual and begin to follow Kyriakos across the hot coals, one by one. Sotiris, the car mechanic, takes his turn and steps in behind Kyriakos on his next dance. Sotiris believes that following Kyriakos gives him strength, and that perhaps one day he himself will be able to lead the others. But as the other participants dance joyfully in a circle around the fire, there is one who is having trouble taking that first step....

---

[13]**skeptic:** a disbelieving or doubtful person

Iro Handjantonieu stands frozen on the edge of the fire, unable to move. Her eyesight is weak, which makes it particularly difficult for her to walk across the coals. Her faith is uncertain, and she is reluctant to believe she will be able to cross the fire unharmed. Others warn her not to cross, saying that doubt and hesitation can lead to serious injury. "You cannot persuade anyone to enter the fire," explains Kyriakos. "If someone isn't ready, they cannot do it."

The dancing continues into the night, but for the weak of heart time is running out. Iro still stands at the edge of the fiery ring, crossing herself and praying. The fire is dying, and it won't be lit again for another year. It will soon be her last chance to take that first step. Finally, Iro calls upon all of her courage and her faith, and hesitatingly begins to dance across the hot coals. She is led by her son, who has come to ensure she is okay. The two dance quickly across the coals, Iro concentrating on reaching her goal. After completing her pass across the coals, Iro is delighted that she managed to overcome her fears. "I didn't think I would do it," she says. "I said my prayers, but they didn't help. My eyesight is so poor these days, so my son led me across." To this the thankful mother adds, "I helped him years ago; he helps me today."

An elderly woman walking across the coals

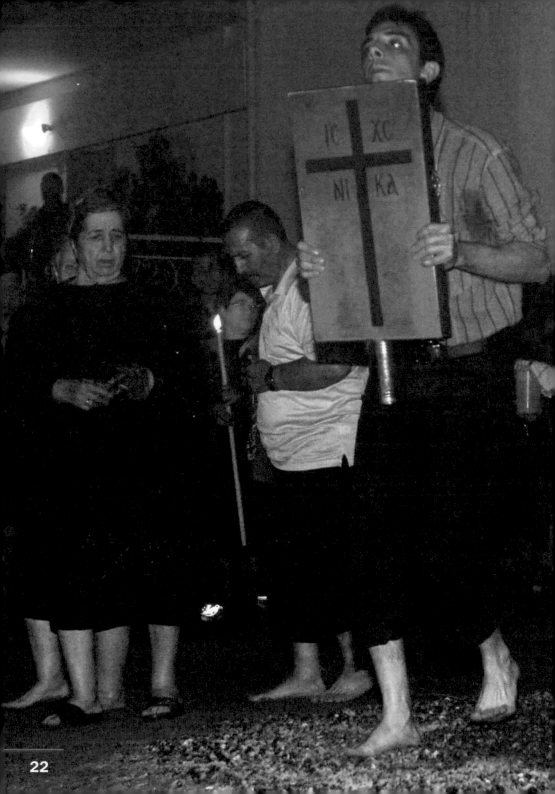

Iro has completed her test of faith, and the ceremony continues until the hot coals are nearly stamped out by the feet of the dancers. The music carries on throughout the evening, and the firewalkers link their arms and dance in a circle around the spot where the fire once was. The atmosphere is a joyful one. Kyriakos, Sotiris, and everyone who managed to walk across the coals are thrilled that their faith carried them through the test. They feel that they have invoked the power and the blessings of Saint Constantine through the act.

Spectators of the ritual have different attitudes about what they have seen. Later, after the firewalkers have left the area, a few members of the crowd watching the ritual move closer to the coals. Some of the skeptics bend down to feel the ground with their hands, perhaps in an attempt to feel if the coals were really that hot. Some of these people may be questioning if they, too, might be capable of walking through fire. Others may be wondering why the firewalkers' feet are not burned. For almost all, the evening's events seem very mysterious, and quite possibly **inexplicable**,[14] however there are others who seek an explanation.

---

[14]**inexplicable:** unable to be explained

Science has offered a number of possible explanations about the physical act of firewalking and as to how practitioners may walk away unhurt. Some hypothesize that sweat from the body forms a layer between the skin and the coals, which protects the skin from being burned. While this or other theories regarding the protection of the firewalkers' feet may be true, they cannot explain everything. As one expert says, while science may be a very powerful way of explaining what happens, it is not necessarily the only way—or in many instances, the most interesting way—to explain things. Some believe that science may explain how something can be done, while faith may explain why one should be able to do it. In the end, faith is a phenomenon that seems to **defy**[15] intellectual inquiry or explanation.

---

[15]**defy:** refuse a rule or natural law; go against

Fact or Opinion?

Look at the following statements. Write 'F' for those that are factual or 'O' for those that are an opinion.

1. Science offers some possible explanations why firewalkers don't get harmed. _____

2. Sweat forms a layer between the skin and coals that protects the feet. _____

3. Science explains how something can be done, while faith explains why one should be able to do it. _____

4. Faith is a phenomenon that seems to defy intellectual inquiry. _____

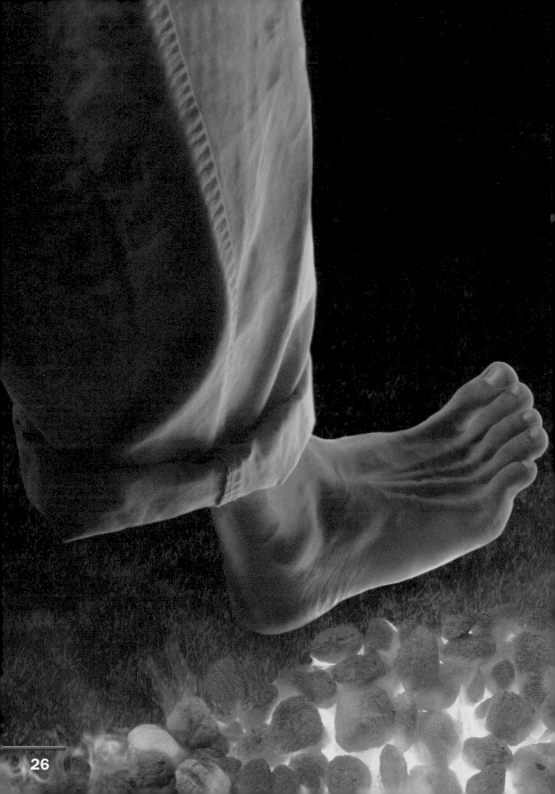

Back at the shrine to Saint Constantine, the faithful firewalkers need no further explanation for what has just happened. They could have been badly burned. But as they hold their feet up for examination, they all seem to be untouched and completely fine. To them, the act of firewalking is about faith. They are convinced that the saint has helped them to take the test of fire and to survive unharmed as their ancestors did.

The participants in the most recent Anastenaria are back with their families, secure in their beliefs after a successful ritual. Sotiris is convinced that his faith—and his readiness to test it—has **prolonged**[16] his life, and given him precious time with the grandson he might never have seen. For the leader, Kyriakos, there's a sense that he has completed his duty to the village. He believes that by taking the test of fire together, the firewalkers have ensured that the community will receive the blessings of Saint Constantine for another year.

[16]**prolong:** make longer; extend

After You Read

1. What claim is NOT made about the festival for Saint Constantine on page 4?
   A. It takes place in the spring.
   B. Icons are carried through the streets.
   C. Worshipers ask for blessings.
   D. Priests walk through fire.

2. The word 'chief' on page 7 is closest in meaning to:
   A. subordinate
   B. primary
   C. civil
   D. liberal

3. The purpose of paragraph 1 on page 8 is to:
   A. provide background information
   B. imply that the icon stories are false
   C. offer a distorted version of history
   D. condemn the beliefs of the worshippers

4. The Greek Orthodox Church considers firewalking to be sacrilege because:
   A. Some icons have been destroyed by it in the past.
   B. The firewalkers are not asking for blessings.
   C. They believe it shows disregard for the icons.
   D. Practitioners consider it to be holy.

5. Sotiris Panagiotou is used as an example of someone:
   A. struggling with the church's condemnation of firewalking
   B. trying to mediate between the church and the firewalkers
   C. positive about unifying the church and the firewalkers
   D. who joined the firewalkers after a personal crisis

6. In paragraph 2 on page 15, the writer implies that people cry while dancing because they:
   A. are fearful of walking over the coals
   B. feel the sorrow of the other dancers
   C. are wrestling with personal guilt
   D. are reluctant to go against the church

7. What does the writer NOT claim about firewalkers on page 16?
   A. A few show indications of pain.
   B. They spend a long time preparing.
   C. They see their ritual as sacred and religious.
   D. Some feel freed from the hierarchy of the church.

8. Some experts believe that the group energy is part of the reason
   _____ firewalkers don't get burned.
   A. for
   B. why
   C. which
   D. if

9. Which of the following questions cannot be answered by the
   information on page 20?
   A. What health issue made it difficult for Iro to cross the coals?
   B. How many people warn Iro not to cross the coals?
   C. What is one reason why Iro was afraid to cross?
   D. Who helps Iro cross the coals?

10. Which of the following verbs on page 23 is closest in meaning
   to 'called on?'
   A. stamped out
   B. managed
   C. invoked
   D. bend down

11. What do some skeptics try to do after the firewalking is finished?
   A. look at the firewalkers' feet
   B. feel the temperature of the coals
   C. demand the firewalkers be given a police citation
   D. handle the religious icons

12. What does the writer probably believe about firewalking?
   A. It shows that faith can't be empirically examined.
   B. It is a pagan ritual.
   C. It is a phenomenon that can be explained by science.
   D. It proves the hypothesis that sweat protects the skin.

Class:	Social Studies
Teacher:	Ms. Klevberg
Assignment:	Write a short report about a cultural tradition.

Fire Rituals in Five Cultures
by Anush Patel

Since the beginning of time, fire has played an important role in the belief systems of people around the world. Although today's fire ceremonies may have modern additions, their origins are thousands of years old. Several cultures continue to honor these ancient rituals even today.

The beginning of spring in Iran is also considered the beginning of the New Year. This holiday is marked by a two-week celebration called *Noruz*, which actually means 'New Day.' On the last Wednesday of *Noruz*, people build fires and jump over them, shouting, "Give me your redness; take back my paleness!" as they symbolically jump out of the old year and into the new spring.

In India, religious ceremonies that involve placing offerings into a fire are called *homas*. The foundation for a *homa* ritual fire is generally made of brick or stone and built in a square shape. The person receiving the benefit sits with spiritual leaders near the fire. The leaders then place ritual offerings into the fire while family and friends form a close circle around them. There are different types of *homas* for different purposes; some are designed to bring financial success, others to increase intelligence.

The Beltane Fire Festival is held annually on the night of April 30th in Edinburgh, Scotland. Its origins are in a pre-Christian celebration of the coming of spring. When farmers took their animals out into the fields for the summer, all the fires in the town were put out, and two sacred fires lit to invoke blessings. As the animals were led between the fires, the heat and smoke were thought to bless the animals and protect them for the year to come.

For Native Americans in the United States, fire ceremonies have always been an important way to ensure the health of body, spirit, and heart. They have often been planned according to the phases of the moon. A fire ceremony is held during the full moon if the person wants to release something from the past, or during the new moon to make a prayer request for something new.

Part of the traditional New Year's celebration for some Filipino couples involves holding each other's hands and jumping over a burning fire. This ritual has its origins in Chinese culture, but is more often celebrated in the Philippines. Like all fire ceremonies, it gets its deepest meaning from the feelings in the hearts of those who participate in it.

A New Year's celebration in the Philippines

CD 2, Track 06

Word Count: 406
Time: _____

Vocabulary List

Christian (3, 4, 15)
coal (2, 3, 8, 12, 15, 16, 17, 19, 20, 21, 23, 24, 25)
confession (15)
cross oneself (4, 16, 20)
defy (24, 25)
descendant (8)
fume (12)
Greek Orthodox (3, 4, 11, 16)
icon (2, 3, 4, 7, 8, 9, 11, 15, 16)
inexplicable (23)
lyre (2, 3, 15)
miraculously (8)
pagan (3, 4, 11)
priest (3, 4)
procession (4, 16)
prolong (27)
quaint (7)
ritual (2, 3, 4, 8, 11, 12, 15, 16, 19, 23, 27)
sacrilegious (3, 4, 11)
saint (2, 3, 4, 5, 8, 9, 12, 15, 16, 19, 23, 27)
shrine (2, 27)
sin (15)
skeptic (19, 23)
touch (one's) heart (15)
worship (3, 4, 8, 15, 17)